Fun to do

PAINT

Jann Haworth

CONTENTS

Swallow

What You Will Need

Before you begin the projects in this book, it is a good idea to collect together some useful tools first. You will need scissors for cutting; a pencil, eraser and ruler for drawing and marking out; and glue for fixing things together. You will need paper to paint onto, and, of course, paint. Turn the page for advice on paint-brushes, as well as some other ideas for putting paint on paper.

scissors

ruler

pencil and eraser

paper

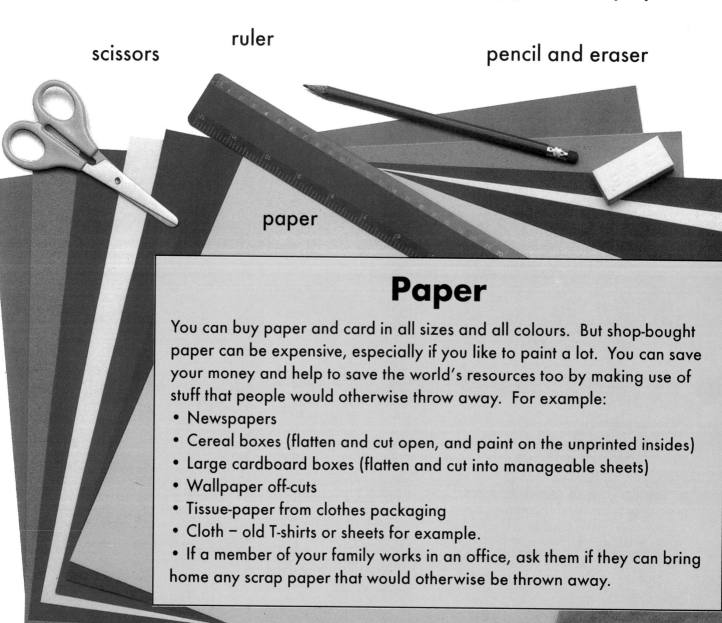

Paper

You can buy paper and card in all sizes and all colours. But shop-bought paper can be expensive, especially if you like to paint a lot. You can save your money and help to save the world's resources too by making use of stuff that people would otherwise throw away. For example:
- Newspapers
- Cereal boxes (flatten and cut open, and paint on the unprinted insides)
- Large cardboard boxes (flatten and cut into manageable sheets)
- Wallpaper off-cuts
- Tissue-paper from clothes packaging
- Cloth – old T-shirts or sheets for example.
- If a member of your family works in an office, ask them if they can bring home any scrap paper that would otherwise be thrown away.

Paint

Water-based paints have been used for all the projects in this book. You can buy them ready-mixed in large, easy-to-use, squeezy bottles. The basic colours you will need are red, yellow, blue, black and white. From these you can mix all other colours, as you will see on page 6. You can use acrylic paints which come in tubes, but do avoid powder paints: they are dusty, difficult to make up and the colours do not mix well.

Add water to paint to make it thinner or PVA glue to make it thicker.

metal ruler

card

string

masking tape

PVA glue

craft knife

felt-tip pens

water-based paint

acrylic paint

wax crayons

oil-based crayons

tissue-paper

Remember

☆ Wear an apron and cover the work area.
☆ Always ask an adult for help when you see this sign ❗
☆ Clear up after yourself.

3

Brush Up On Painting

When you begin to paint, you will need to paint with something. The first thing you might think of is a paint-brush, but there are lots of other things you could use. Blow puddles of thin paint around with a straw. Use your fingers, hands or cut vegetables to print with. Make a card comb and twist it through thick paint, or dabble and smear paint on with a rag. Draw with a twig dipped in thin paint. Last but not least, look at all the different kinds of brushes you could use and try them out for yourself.

plastic comb

plastic straws

twig

card comb

cut potato

roller

hands

newspaper

Useful Things to Collect

All sorts of things around the home can be used to print paint onto paper. Why not make a collection. Here are some ideas to start you off:

Corrugated card, bubble pack, corks, cotton reels, sponges, cotton wadding, jars with the labels still on, leaves, cut fruit and vegetables, off-cuts of wood, cloth, old shoes, boxes, etc.

cloths

decorating brushes

paint-brushes

toothbrush

nail-brush

scrubbing brush

shaving brush

5

Colour Mixing

What colour will it make? All you will need is a basic set of paints (see page 3), a white plate and a brush to find out!

Mix red and yellow to make orange. Add more red for a warmer orange and more yellow for a tangerine shade.

Blue and yellow mixed together makes green. You can vary the shade by adding more or less yellow or blue.

Mix a brushful of red with a drop of blue. Now try a drop of red with a brushful of blue. How is it different?

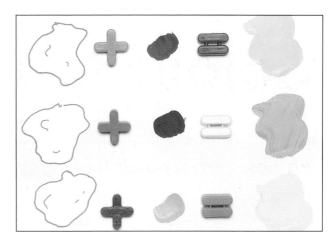

Red and green mixed together makes brown. Now try orange and blue.

To make pastel colours, simply add a drop of any coloured paint to white paint.

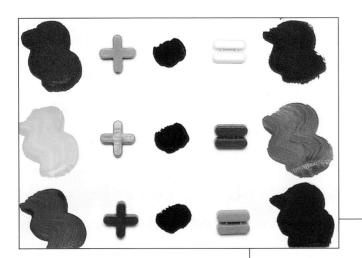

Now see what happens when you mix a drop of black to any colour.

Skin tones are harder to mix. Here are a couple of examples. Now try to mix a colour to match your skin.

Sqeeze small amounts of paint onto an old saucer or plate, or even a thick piece of card. Use a brush to mix them together.

What an Effect

Have a go at using some of the tools on pages 4 and 5 to explore these painting techniques.

Dry brush

Put a little paint onto the tip of a dry brush and work it into the bristles by brushing lightly on newspaper. Now paint onto paper – try adding other colours.

Stippling

Cut out a shape from paper and place onto a sheet of card. Dab around the edges of the cut-out shape with a lightly-painted brush.

Rolling and combing

1 Roll a thick layer of paint onto a sheet of card. If you do not have a roller, use a jar with the label still on it.

2 Make a comb by cutting teeth along one edge of a square of thick card. Drag and twist the comb through the paint.

Splattering

Dip a toothbrush into some watered-down paint. Run a paint-brush handle along its bristles to splatter the paint onto the paper. What effect will you get with a nail-brush?

Newspaper crumple

Screw a piece of newspaper into a crumpled ball. Dab into paint and print onto paper. Use other balls of crumpled paper to add more colours.

IN THE FRAME
Frame your pictures as you paint them. Cut 2 L-shaped pieces of thick card. Position these onto the paper so that they mark off a rectangular area. Paint within this area and then remove the card pieces for an instant frame.

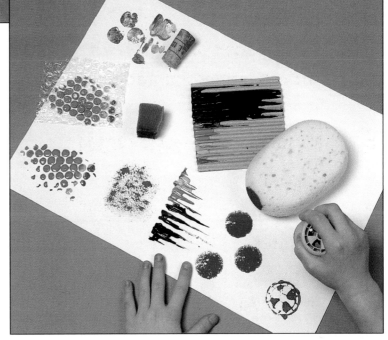

You can use all sorts of things collected from around the house to paint with. Now see what you can find.

The Background Story

Why use only plain paper to draw or paint on when you can create an interesting textured background?

Streaking and dripping

Dip a middle-sized decorating brush into watered-down paint and hold the brush at the top of the paper. Lift the paper and let the paint drip down.

Washes

Dip a large decorating brush into watered-down paint and brush across the paper. Now add different coloured washes, letting the colours run into each other.

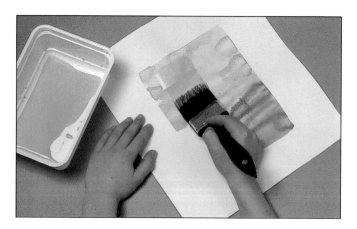

Tonking

1 Paint thickly onto a sheet of paper. Cover an area of the painted paper with newspaper and flatten with your hand.

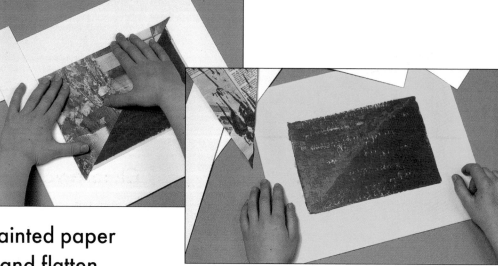

2 Carefully lift off the newspaper.

Rag rolling

1 Put a rag into a tray of paint and stir until it is well covered. Gather into a wrinkled sausage. Place at the bottom left-hand corner of the paper and roll up.

2 Continue to roll the rag in columns across the paper. If the rag print becomes faint, dip the rag in paint again.

Staining

!1 You can use all sorts of household products to stain white paper, for example shoe polish, turmeric, vinegar, coffee, food colouring and soya sauce. Make up a sample sheet like the one in the photograph.

2 Choose your favourite one and stain some sheets of white paper for future paintings. This tea wash is used as a background for the next project in this book.

Me! Me! Me!

A good place to start painting is with a portrait of yourself.

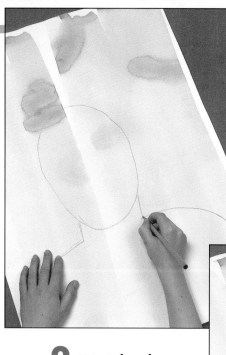

1 Take a textured sheet of paper. Sit in front of a mirror and look at the shape of your face. Draw the outline of it in the centre of the paper.

2 Divide the face up into quarters by marking in light pencil lines horizontally and vertically.

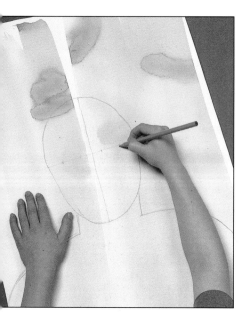

3 Divide the horizontal or eyeline into fifths, to give you a guide for positioning the corners of the eyes.

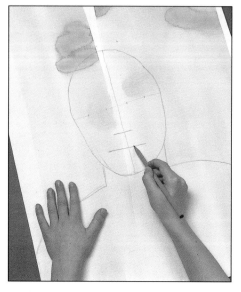

4 Mark in lines for the nose and mouth on the bottom half of the vertical line.

5 Look at your face again. Use the pencil guidelines to help you draw what you see. Rub out these lines when you are happy with your drawing.

6 Before beginning to paint over your drawing make a copy of it. Tape it onto a window and place a sheet of paper on top of it. Trace off your drawing.

7 Paint over your original drawing. Try to match the colour of your eyes and hair. Mark in any freckles. Don't forget your eyebrows and eyelashes.

Trace copies from your original to make countless versions of yourself.

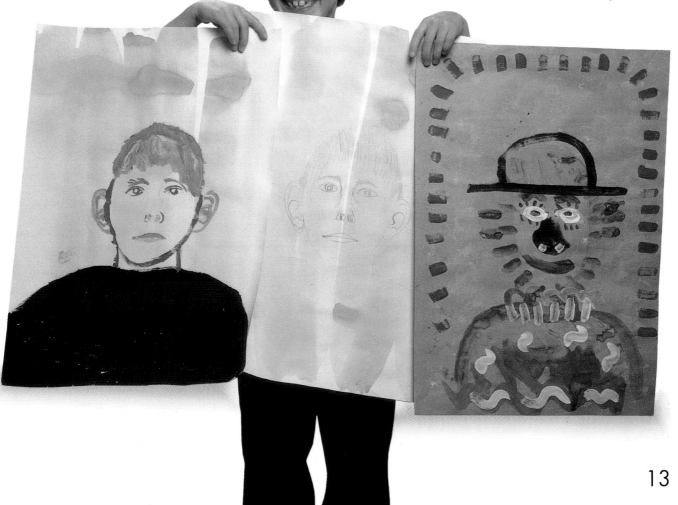

Fruit and Vegetable Printing

Instead of painting a still life of a bowl of fruit, use the fruit (and some vegetables too) to paint the picture!

! **1** Ask your mum or dad if you can have a selection of fruit and vegetables to paint with.

! **2** Now ask your parent if he or she could cut up the fruit and vegetables so that you can print with them.

3 Put out the colours you will need onto a plate. Paint the cut end of a vegetable and begin to print a border around a large sheet of paper.

4 The painted edge of a carrot stick has been used to print this bowl and the table mat beneath it.

14

5 An apple cut in half and painted has been used to print different coloured apples in the bowl.

6 The round end of a carrot has been used to build up a bunch of grapes. A half a lemon has been used to print an orange. The round end of a carrot painted red makes the cherries.

You can have great fun experimenting with the variety of effects that can be achieved with this simple printing technique.

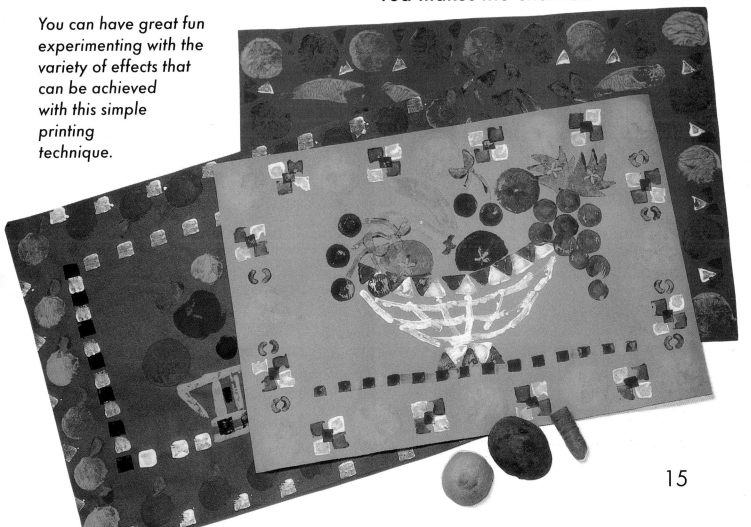

Tree of Life Stencil

A *stencil is made by cutting a pattern from a piece of card or paper. It can then be painted over to reproduce the same pattern as many times as you like.*

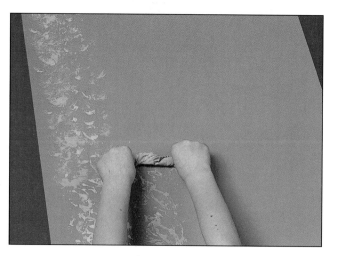

1 Rag roll over a sheet of paper using a slightly lighter shade of paint than the colour of the paper. Leave to dry.

2 To make the trunk and branches of the tree, paint your hand and forearm brown and print at the bottom of the paper.

3 Draw half shapes of leaves, butterflies, hearts, flowers and stars along the folded line of some small squares of white paper. Cut out the shapes and open up the paper. These are your stencils.

4 Put a stencil on the ragged paper. Stipple the paint all over the stencil. Take care that the paint does not creep under the edge of the stencil.

5 Fill out the shape of the tree by building up a pattern of stencils across the paper. Leave to dry.

The finished picture. Now make several versions. Cut more stencils – try varying the shapes of the leaves.

6 To add some detail to your picture, cut a leaf vein stencil from paper. Place the stencil over the painted leaves and stipple with black paint.

Draw With Glue

A picture drawn with glue makes a wonderful printing block.

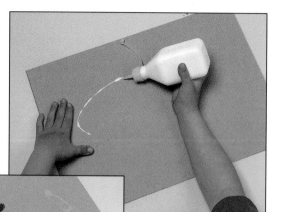

1 Use glue to draw a picture onto a piece of thick card. Leave to dry overnight.

2 When the glue has dried completely, colour in the areas between the lines with wax or oil-based crayons.

3 Paint all over the surface of the card. Work fast so that the paint does not dry.

4 Lay a sheet of white tissue-paper over the painted card and smooth down with your hands. Carefully peel back the tissue-paper.

5 Put the tissue-paper print to one side to dry.

18

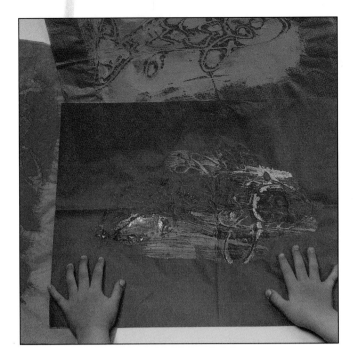

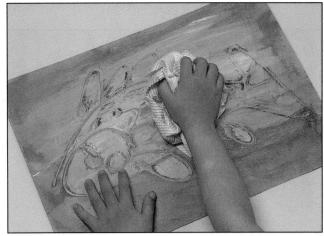

6 Paint all over the card again. This time make a print onto a coloured sheet of tissue-paper. You can make as many prints of your picture as you like.

7 When you have made all the prints you want, use a damp cloth to wipe most of the paint off the card. Leave some paint in the corners. When you have finished, the colour of the crayons should be showing through brightly again.

The printing card has become a picture in itself. Make a frame for it and hang it on the wall.

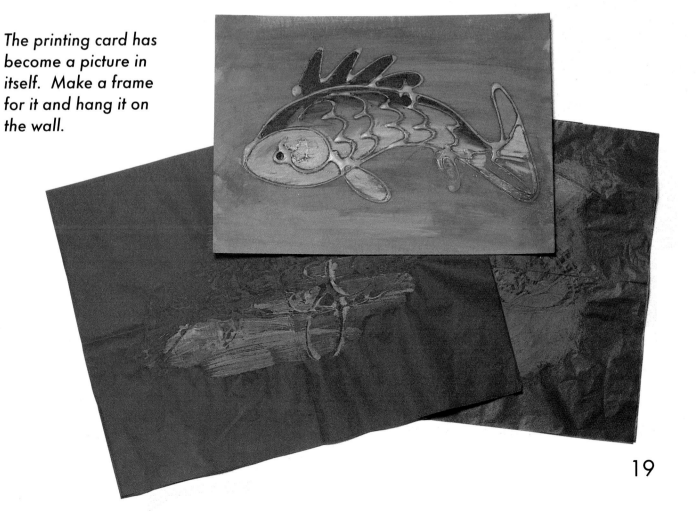

19

Cloth Printing

Transform an old sheet with a little paint and a simple printing block made from card.

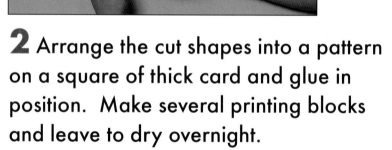

Materials

newspapers

thick card

cloth

! 1 Cut out a variety of shapes from thick card.

2 Arrange the cut shapes into a pattern on a square of thick card and glue in position. Make several printing blocks and leave to dry overnight.

! 3 Cut out a 60 cm x 60 cm square of cloth, iron and place on a bed of newspaper (6–8 layers) ready for printing onto. Quickly apply a thick layer of paint to a printing block.

4 Press the block down hard on the bottom edge of the cloth. Print another square next to the first, and so on.

! 5 As the print fades, put more paint on the block. Build up a pyramid of printed squares. When the paint has dried, place the cloth upside down on the newspaper and iron.

! 6 Prepare another piece of cloth. Paint 2 printing blocks different colours and use in turn to print rows of squares.

7 To make table mats, cut out the printed squares. Make a fringe by pulling out the threads along the edges of the cloth.

Ask an adult to help you sew together 2 pieces of printed cloth to make a cushion cover.

FABRIC PAINTS
If you use ordinary paint for printing, the things you make from the printed cloth will not be washable. You can buy special fabric paints from an art shop that can be washed. These are used in exactly the same way.

21

String Pictures

In this project you will use string to draw with, print with and to make a decorative frame.

Materials

shells

string

thick card

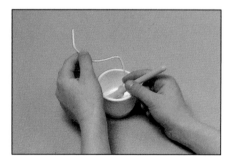

1 Put a long piece of string into a cupful of glue and stir it around.

2 Take the string out of the glue and pull it through your fingers so that it does not drip everywhere.

3 Lay the string on top of a small square of card (12 cm x 12 cm) to make a picture. You may need to cut the string into small pieces. Leave your string picture to dry overnight.

4 Lay paper onto a bed of newspaper. Paint over the string picture and press down hard onto the paper. Make several prints.

5 Choose your favourite print and frame it. Put the string picture in the centre of a large square of card (17 cm x 17 cm), draw around it and lift it off.

6 Decorate the border by drawing on a pattern with glue-covered string. Stick on some shells. Leave overnight to dry.

7 Colour in the spaces around the string and the shells with wax or oil-based crayons.

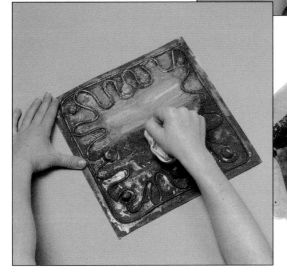

8 To give the frame an antique effect, paint all over the card with brown paint. Use a rag to dab off some of the paint.

Cut a print down to fit into the centre of the frame. Glue into place. Ask an adult to hang it up for you.

23

Painter's Sketchbook

Make this book to keep your favourite pictures in.

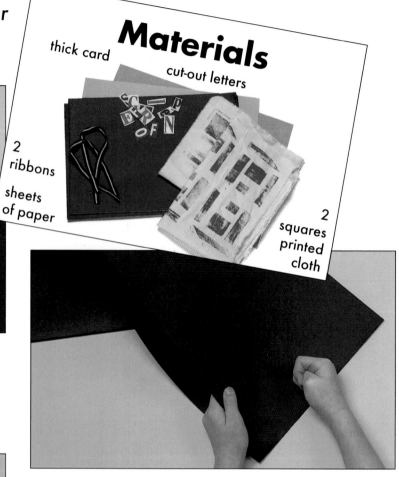

Materials

thick card

cut-out letters

2 ribbons

sheets of paper

2 squares printed cloth

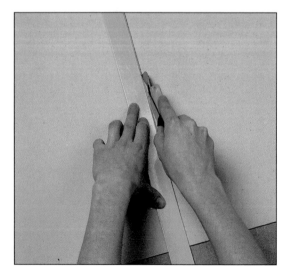

1 Make a long strip of paper by gluing several sheets of paper end to end.

2 Fold evenly into a zig zag.

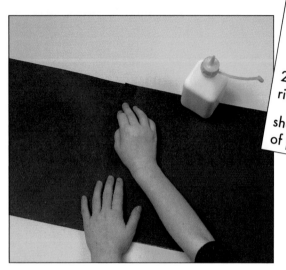

⚠ 3 Cut 2 pieces of thick card about 1 cm larger all around than the folded zig zag of paper.

4 Now cover both pieces of card with the printed cloth made on page 20.

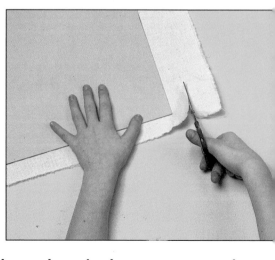

Place the card on the cloth. Cut around the fabric leaving a 2.5 cm edge.

5 Use a brush to dampen the edges of the cloth with water.

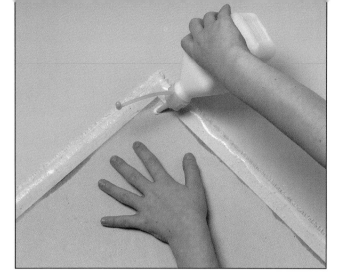

6 Run a line of glue all around the edge of the cloth and a blob on each corner of the card.

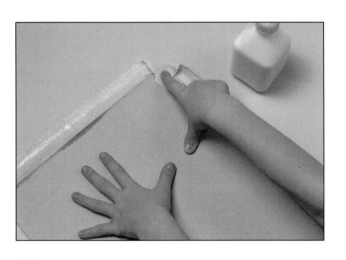

7 Fold the corners of the cloth over onto the card as shown.

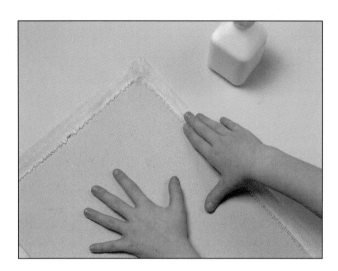

8 Fold over the sides of the cloth as shown. Make sure that the corner seams do not overlap each other, and check that the fabric is pulled tight across the front of the card.

9 Glue a length of ribbon onto each piece of card.

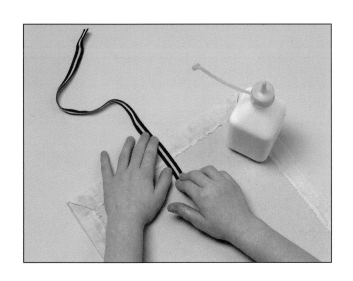

Continues on next page

10 Evenly spread a thin layer of glue over both pieces of card.

11 Run a thin line of glue close to the edge of the first page of the zig zag strip of paper. Press the paper onto a piece of covered card.

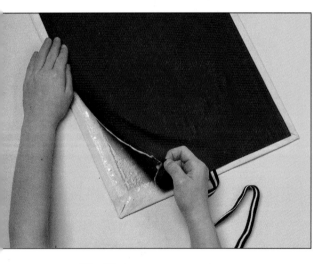

12 Glue around the last page of the zig zag strip and press onto the second piece of covered card. Make sure that the ribbons are both on the same side so they can be tied together.

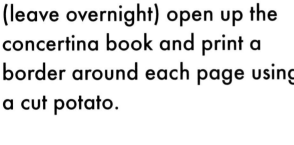

13 Once the glue has dried (leave overnight) open up the concertina book and print a border around each page using a cut potato.

Fill your book with your favourite pictures painted by you, your family and your friends. When it is full, make a present of it to a friend.

14 Cut out letters from magazine or newspaper headlines and make a title for your book.

Fresco

Paint a picture onto the plaster surface of a small sheet of plasterboard and hang it on the wall. Plasterboard is cheap and can be bought from any DIY shop.

1 Use a large decorating brush to cover both sides of the plasterboard with water. Leave overnight to dry.

2 Mark out a large rectangle on the front of the board leaving an even frame all around.

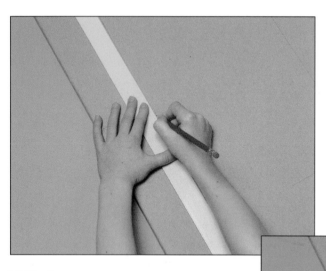

! **3** Ask an adult to cut through the paper along the marked lines just into the plaster below.

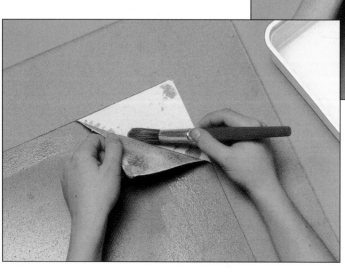

4 Carefully peel back the paper to reveal the plaster below. If the paper does not come away cleanly, run a wet paint-brush under the edge.

28

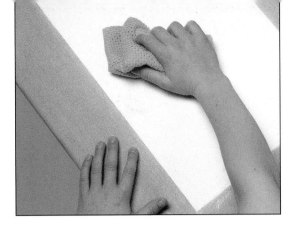

5 Scrub the plaster with a damp cloth. Scrap off any remaining patches of paper with a round-ended knife. Don't worry if the surface of the plaster looks scratched or pitted. This will give a more interesting effect when painted over.

6 Paint a picture onto the plaster using watered-down paint. Try a portrait of your mum or dad, or your pet.

7 Use stencils cut from thin card to decorate the paper frame. Use a thick brush to stipple the paint onto the stencil, taking care not to let paint creep under the edge.

Furniture Painting

An old piece of furniture can be transformed by your imagination and just a little paint. But do ask mum or dad for permission first.

1 Use fine sandpaper to rub down the area of wood to be painted.

2 Put a little washing-up liquid into a bowl of warm water and wash down the sanded wood. Leave to dry.

3 Sketch out a rough design for the area to be painted. This is just a guide, and you can change it as you work.

4 Cut all the stencils you will need from thin card.

5 Work outwards from the centre of your design. Tape the stencil to the wood.

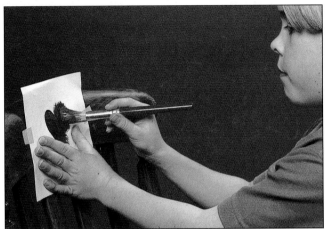

6 Use a thick brush to dab paint over the stencil.

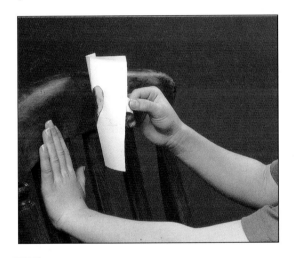

⚠ **7** Carefully peel off the stencil. Build up your design using one stencil at a time. Once the paint has dried ask an adult to help you brush the painted area with a thin coat of varnish.

The finished chair. Now everyone will want to sit on it.

Advice to Parents

Most of the projects in this book take between 5 and 10 minutes to set up and perhaps the same amount of time to clean up. In between is an experience that every child needs. Although children do painting at school, the time and materials they have may be limited, and it may be difficult for them to work undisturbed. For children to explore the rich experience of painting they need room to stretch out, time to think, and the opportunity to explore. They also need someone who will praise them unreservedly as only a parent can, and they need to see their pictures displayed around the home. I've been painting since I was a little girl and I think the most important factor in this has been the interest of my parents and family. I hope the information in this book will help you and your child to discover and enjoy painting together.

What Do You Need to Provide

All that is required from you is an area of floor space where the child can work undisturbed, paint, a few basic tools and your interest and encouragement. When compared with the cost of modern toys and games, painting is a cheap, fun and constructive way for children to occupy their time. So don't be put off by the setting up and clearing away of the activity. It only takes a few minutes.

Making space

Lay an old sheet down on the floor in a corner of the room where the child will not be in anybody's way. Lay newspaper on top. Try to stay in the room with your child so that he can show you his work as he develops it. If you set up in a corner of the kitchen, do make sure that the child is nowhere near the cooker.

Clearing up

You can minimize the mess by making sure the work space is well covered *and* by covering up your child before they begin work. Buy a wipe-clean plastic apron, or make a painting smock out of an old shirt – simply cut off the collar and cuffs and sew some elastic in in their place.

Encourage your child to help you clean up afterwards. Wash paint pots and brushes out well so that they are ready for use next time. Store the dry brushes bristle end up in a pot or jar.

Materials and Tools

Some of the things your child might need are mentioned on pages 2–5 of this book. Here is some additional advice you should bear in mind.

• Glue: Solvent-free PVA adhesive is recommended as it is versatile, clean, strong and safe.

• Scissors: For the sake of safety children should use small scissors with round-ended metal blades and plastic handles. Although these are fine for cutting paper and thin card, they will not cut thick card and this is best done by you. This will often require a craft knife. Use a metal ruler to provide a straight cutting edge. If you do not have a cutting mat, use an old chopping board or very thick card to protect the work surface beneath.

• Varnish: When painting furniture the surface is sealed with a light coat of varnish. Children should be carefully supervised when using varnish. Cover the work surface with newspaper, use in a well-ventilated room, clean brushes immediately after use with white spirits, and store the varnish carefully as it is a flammable material.

• Paper: Paper can be expensive to buy, so do make a point of trying to re-use it wherever possible. Save cereal packets, old cardboard boxes, newspapers, clothes packaging, wallpaper off-cuts, out-of-date calendars – any paper in fact that would otherwise be thrown away.

• Paint: Always have the basic set of colours in stock: red, blue, yellow, black and white. All other colours can be mixed from these. Provide your child with an old plate to mix paint on. Buy ready-mixed water-based paint in the economy washing-up bottle size. These last for ages, they mix well, and the child will not be discouraged by thin or lumpy paint.

The End Product

There is no right way to paint. Art is experimenting, seeing what happens and finding out how. An interesting picture may not always look 'nice'. Don't worry if your child's picture doesn't look like anything, or if it looks messy, or even if your child has 'messed up' an earlier 'better' picture – the most important thing is that she is experimenting. When your child has finished a picture, get her to say what she does or does not like about the picture. Asking questions will help her to develop her ideas next time.

Do remember that all the designs for the projects in this book are simply offered as guidelines. They are not meant to be copied. Encourage your child to develop her own ideas and to be proud of what she achieves.

My grateful thanks to my mother, Miriam Haworth, and my daughter, Libby Blake,
for their hard work helping me to produce this book.
Jann Haworth 1993

Swallow is an imprint of Merehurst Limited
Reprinted 1996 by Merehurst Limited
Ferry House, 51-57 Lacy Road, Putney, London SW15 1PR

© Copyright 1993 Merehurst Limited
ISBN 1 898018 05 7

Project Editor: Cheryl Brown
Designer: Anita Ruddell
Photography by Jon Bouchier
Colour separation by Scantrans Pte Limited, Singapore
Printed in Italy by G. Canale & C.,S.p.A.

The publisher would like to thank the staff and children of Riversdale Primary School, London Borough of Wandsworth, The Early Learning Centre, Phoebe Wood-Wheelhouse, Allie Johnstone, Lewis Elwin and Jay Darlington for their help in producing the photographs for this book.